About Your Theme Calendar

Planned Theme Play

Young children learn through play. Planned theme play can enhance regular play by providing opportunities for children to make connections and to see relationships. It can also stimulate children's brain development by having them use multiple senses when making discoveries about a specific topic.

With planned theme play, the themes serve as fun vehicles for helping children acquire important thinking skills.

Planned theme play also helps children understand that all learning is connected—that they can learn about a topic in many different ways. For instance, they can explore the subject of caterpillars by observing a live one, by singing a caterpillar song, by making a pretend caterpillar out of modeling dough, by moving like a caterpillar, and so forth.

Learning Through Themes

When you offer young children multisensory age-appropriate activities structured around a central theme, you can be assured of early learning success.

Themes offer the opportunity to:

☆ integrate learning experiences.

☆ allow children to repeat basic skills in a variety of ways.

☆ incorporate the use of multiple senses, thus ensuring understanding, no matter what a child's dominant learning style may be.

☆ engage children and adults in quality learning time.

Your *Theme Calendar* incorporates activities that have been designed to develop the following skills.

Language skills—activities involving rhymes, stories, and puppet play.

Creative art and problem-solving skills—activities that foster making choices and decisions.

Coordination skills—activities that use large and small muscles.

Music skills—activities that incorporate songs, rhymes, and rhythms—all helpful for later development of reading and math skills.

Thinking and beginning math skills—activities that deal with relationships, basic shapes, size, positions, sorting and matching, and likes and differences.

Jean Warren

Using Your Theme Calendar

☆ At the beginning of each week, look through the activities to get an overview of the contents.

☆ If a week's theme would work better for you at a different time of year, just switch weeks, substituting one for the other.

☆ Plan to do the activities spread out over the week, or do them all together, if you wish.

☆ Pick and choose the activities you think you and your child will enjoy doing.

☆ Feel free to adapt any of the activities to fit your child's age and ability, or your particular situation.

☆ As you work on an activity together, encourage conversation about what your child is doing and sensing.

☆ If your child has difficulty with an activity, don't worry. Just try another one you think is more suitable.

☆ Look for opportunities to extend the week's theme by including your own and your child's experiences that relate to the topic.

☆ Remember that having fun promotes the best learning. And working with themes keeps learning fun!

January

Crawl, Crawl

Sung to: "The Paw-Paw Patch"

Crawl, crawl on your blanket.

Crawl, crawl on your blanket.

Crawl, crawl on your blanket.

Crawl, little Alex,

On your blanket now.

Substitute such words as *roll* or *squirm* for *crawl*, and your child's name for *Alex*.

Elizabeth McKinnon

My Blanket

Ask your child to find his favorite blanket. Help him talk about how it looks and feels. Then take a photo of him and his "blankie," and display it where he can easily see it.

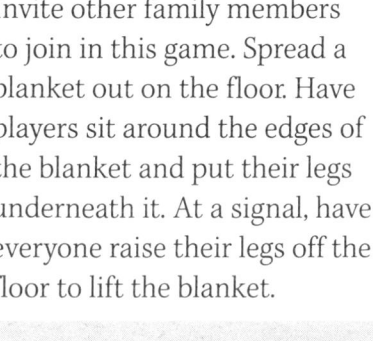

Picnic Blanket

Sit with your child on a blanket and enjoy a simple picnic lunch.

Blanket Lift

Invite other family members to join in this game. Spread a blanket out on the floor. Have players sit around the edges of the blanket and put their legs underneath it. At a signal, have everyone raise their legs off the floor to lift the blanket.

Blanket Tent

Create a tent by draping a blanket over a small table or between two pieces of furniture. Add a pillow or a stuffed toy, and invite your child to play inside the Blanket Tent.

Little Blanket

I have a little blanket,

It's soft as soft can be.

And when I go

To Grandma's house,

My blanket goes with me.

Substitute other names for *Grandma*.

Elizabeth McKinnon

Blanket Peekaboo

Let your child hide under a blanket. Pretend that he has disappeared, then quickly lift the blanket to find him. Or, pull the blanket off slowly as you say, "Oh, I've found a leg! Oh my, I've found another leg!" and so forth.

Big Hand, Little Hand

Fingerpaint with your child on separate pieces of paper. On another paper, make your handprint next to your child's handprint. Which hand is bigger? Which is smaller?

Finger Foods

Throughout the week, serve finger foods as snacks. Your child is sure to enjoy such treats as dry cereal pieces, cheese cubes, tiny crackers, or finger gelatin.

Hand Picture

Use a crayon to trace around your child's hand on a piece of white paper. Invite her to color the paper with watercolors or washable markers. Surprise! Her hand outline still shows through.

Open, Shut Them

Open, shut them,

Open, shut them,

Let your hands go clap.

Open, shut them,

Open, shut them,

Put them in your lap.

Show your child how to use her hands to act out the movements in the rhyme.

Adapted Traditional

Hello, Mr. Hand

Turn your hand into a puppet by drawing a face on your palm with a washable marker. Use your hand puppet to talk to your child or to tell her stories.

Mitten Mates

Put several pairs of mittens into a box and mix them up. Help your child put on one mitten. Can she find its mate? Play the game again, starting with a different mitten.

Wave Your Hands

Sung to: "Row, Row, Row Your Boat"

Wave, wave, wave your hands
  (*Sing slowly.*)
As slowly as can be.

Wave, wave, wave your hands,

Wave them now with me.

Wave, wave, wave your hands
  (*Sing fast.*)
As fast as fast can be.

Wave, wave, wave your hands,

Do it now with me.

Substitute other words, such as *clap* or *rub*, for *wave*.

Adapted Traditional

January

Snowflakes Everywhere

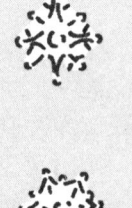

See the snowflakes
Dance around.
See the snowflakes
Touch the ground.
See the snowflakes
In the air.
See the snowflakes
Everywhere!

Encourage your child to dance his fingers like falling snowflakes as you recite the rhyme.

Jean Warren

Snowball Toss

After a snowfall, line up several plastic containers outdoors on a low ledge. Help your child make snowballs and toss them at the containers to try knocking them over.

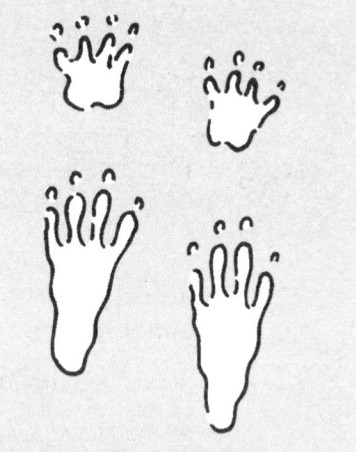

Making Tracks

On fresh snow, look for small animal or bird tracks with your child. Encourage him to walk and run over the snow to make his own tracks. Then invite him to follow the tracks he made, stepping in his own footprints.

Snow Melt

Help your child fill a small plastic container with snow and bring it indoors. Ask him to check the container now and then. What is happening to the snow? What is snow made of?

Snowflake Picture

Tear cotton balls into small pieces. Show your child how to dip the pieces into glue and stick them onto a sheet of blue construction paper to make fluffy snowflakes.

Snow Story

Give your child a snow globe to hold. Invite him to gently rock it back and forth as you tell a story about the scene inside.

Little Snowflakes

Sung to: "Frère Jacques"

Little snowflakes,
Little snowflakes,
Twirling round,
Twirling round.
Falling very softly,
Falling very softly
To the ground,
To the ground.

Pretend to be falling snowflakes as you sing.

Diane Thom

Paper Towel Pictures

Cover a table with newspapers and lay out white paper towels. Let your child draw on the towels with water-based markers. Then spray the towels with water and watch as the colors mix and blend.

Paper Towel Roll

Invite your child to lie on the floor, pretending to be a roll of paper towels. Encourage her to roll in one direction to "unwind" and to roll the other way to "wind up."

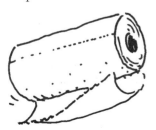

Cleaning Up Drips

I'm tearing off

A paper towel,

Listen to it zip.
> *(Tear off towel.)*

Now my towel

Is ready

To clean up some drips.
> *(Wipe with towel.)*

Elizabeth McKinnon

Cleanup Time

Let your child help you do some housecleaning. Spray items, such as windows, tables, or chairs, with a little water and have her use paper towels to scrub the items clean. While she works, sing "I Am Scrubbing."

Paper Towel Napkins

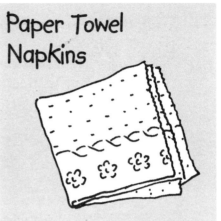

When it's time for a snack, let your child help fold paper towels to use as napkins.

Storytime Fun

Cut familiar shapes or story characters out of thick, fluffy paper towels. Use the shapes on a flannelboard or a textured furniture cushion to tell stories to your child.

I Am Scrubbing

Sung to: "If You're Happy and You Know It"

I am scrubbing all the windows;

Watch me now.

I am scrubbing all the windows;

I know how.

I am scrubbing high and low,

I am scrubbing fast and slow.

I am scrubbing all the windows;

Watch me now.

Substitute the name of the item your child is cleaning for *windows*.

Gayle Bittinger

February

Red Day

Have a Red Day with your child. Celebrate by wearing red clothes, reading a book about red, playing with red toys, going on a walk to look for red, and so forth.

Red Collage

Cut red pictures out of magazines and collect red collage materials, such as scraps of paper and fabric, yarn pieces, rickrack, or plastic straws. Invite your child to glue the pictures and materials onto a piece of red construction paper to make a Red Collage.

Red Snackers

Throughout the week, snack on foods that are red, such as strawberries, red apple slices, tomato soup, or cranberry juice.

Red Touch

Attach a small red sticker to your child's finger. Invite him to walk around the room with you and touch his finger to various red objects.

What Is It?

Hide a small red item, such as a crayon or a toy car, inside a red sock or mitten. Ask your child to feel the outside of the sock and try to guess what the item inside is. Then let him hide a red item in the sock for you to guess.

Red-Nose Clowns

Attach a red circle sticker to your nose and one to your child's nose. Then pretend to be funny clowns and run, jump, waddle, and tumble around the room. For added fun, turn on some music to accompany your clown antics.

I Love the Color Red

Sung to: "The Farmer in the Dell"

I love the color red,

I love the color red.

Red, red, my shoes are red.

I love the color red.

Continue singing about other things that are red.

Elizabeth McKinnon

Hearts Everywhere

Hearts on the cake,

Hearts on the box,

Hearts on the shoes,

Hearts on the socks.

Hearts on the table,

Hearts on the chair,

Hearts on the wall,

Hearts everywhere!

Hearts *are* everywhere this time of year! Encourage your child to point out those she sees.

Jean Warren

Red Hearts

Sung to: "Row, Row, Row Your Boat"

One, two, three red hearts,

Pretty as can be.

See them standing in a row,

Just for you and me.

Sing while counting heart stickers or paper hearts.

Elizabeth McKinnon

Heart Lineup

Cut four or five hearts of various sizes out of red construction paper. Mix them up and give them to your child. Invite her to line up the hearts from smallest to largest or from largest to smallest.

Heart Hop

Cut heart shapes out of construction paper and tape them to the floor. Then put on some music and invite your child to hop like a bunny from one heart to another.

Pass the Heart

Cut a heart shape out of red construction paper. Sit with your child and pass the heart back and forth as you name people you love.

Grandma Daddy
Grandpa
Auntie Mary
Jason

Valentine Hearts

Cut heart shapes out of white or pink construction paper. Give your child a washable red ink pad and let her decorate the hearts with her fingerprints or thumbprints. Encourage her to give her hearts as valentines.

Strawberry Heart

Let your child use a plastic knife to spread softened cream cheese on a piece of bread or a cracker. Give her half a strawberry to place cut-side down on top of the cheese, helping her to see how the strawberry half looks like a small heart.

February

Blanket Pull

Place a small blanket on the floor and put a stuffed animal or similar toy on one end. Invite your child to pick up the other end of the blanket and pull the toy around the room.

Jingly Sock Pull

Tuck several jingle bells into the toe of a long tube sock and fill the rest of the sock with lightly crumpled paper. Use a short piece of ribbon to tie the sock closed. Show your child how to pull the sock around by the ribbon to make the bells jingle.

Push Cars

Make a simple road by attaching masking tape to the floor. Encourage your child to choose toy cars and have fun pushing them along the road.

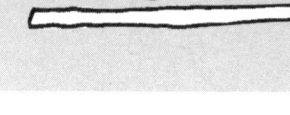

Tractor Push

Place books or magazines in a cardboard carton and securely tape it shut. Ask your child to make believe the box is a giant rock that must be moved. Let him pretend to be a tractor and push the box around the room.

Push & Pull Toys

Show your child how to push and pull various toys. Then invite him to play with the toys, encouraging him to tell you if he is pushing or pulling them.

Push & Pull Basket

Tie a short, sturdy cord handle to one end of a laundry basket. Invite your child to place several stuffed animals inside. Then give him directions such as, "Push the toys over to the window" or "Now pull the toys around the room."

I Push and Pull

Sung to: "Three Blind Mice"

Push and pull,
Push and pull.
Pull and push,
Pull and push.
I push my truck
Across the floor.
I pull my wagon
Out the door.
I push and pull
And push some more.
Push and pull.

Substitute the names of your child's toys for *truck* and *wagon*.

Gayle Bittinger

Dancing Spoon

Sung to: "The Muffin Man"

Come and see

My dancing spoon,

My dancing spoon,

My dancing spoon.

Come and see

My dancing spoon

As round and round

It goes.

Give your child a Spoon Puppet to dance around as you sing.

Jean Warren

Spoon Painting

Pour tempera paint into a bowl and add salt for texture. Place a spoonful of the paint on heavy paper and let your child push it around using the back of the spoon. Add more paint to her paper as needed.

Spoon Puppet

To make a puppet, draw a face in the bowl of a small plastic spoon. At the neck, fasten a paper napkin for a shirt. Then dance the puppet around as you sing "Dancing Spoon."

Stirring Fun

Stirring our soup,

Stirring it slow,

Stirring and stirring,

Around we go.

As you recite the rhyme, walk in a circle, pretending to be spoons stirring a big pot of soup.

Elizabeth McKinnon

Big Spoons, Little Spoons

Put small and large tableware spoons in a basket or box. Invite your child to sort them into two piles by size. Which are the big spoons? Which are the small ones?

Measuring Spoons

Give your child four different measuring spoons. Invite her to line them up from smallest to largest or from largest to smallest. Also encourage her to nest them one inside another.

Snack Spoon

Serve yogurt or a similar snack and set out several different spoons. Let your child choose one to be her special spoon for eating her snack.

March

Wind Watch

Take your child outdoors on a windy day to watch as the wind makes trees, bushes, and other things sway back and forth. Can he point to where he "sees" the wind? What does the wind sound like? What does it feel like?

Paper Bag Kite

Let your child decorate a paper lunch bag with crayons. Punch two holes near the top of the bag, on opposites sides, and tie each end of a piece of string to one of the holes, to make a handle. Outdoors, invite your child to run with his kite to make it "fly" in the wind.

The Wind Is Blowing

Sung to: "The Farmer in the Dell"

The wind is blowing here,

The wind is blowing there.

The wind is blowing all around,

It's blowing everywhere.

Sing with your child on a windy day.
Elizabeth McKinnon

Wind Chime

Hold up a wind chime and encourage your child to make it ring by moving the chimes with his hands. Ask him to try blowing on the chimes to make music. If possible, hang the chime outdoors on a windy day.

Wind Dance

Tape strips of newspaper or crepe paper to your child's wrists and let him dance around the room, pretending to be the wind. Encourage him to sway and swirl as he blows here and there.

Like the Wind

On a bare floor, place a few light and heavy objects, such as a feather, a cotton ball, a rock, and a metal spoon. Let your child try moving the objects the way the wind does by blowing on them. Which objects blow away? Which don't? Why?

Wind Tricks

The wind is full

Of tricks today.

It blew our

Newspaper away.

It chased the trash can

Down the street,

And almost blew us

Off our feet!

What other "wind tricks" has your child seen?

Adapted Traditional

Feet, Feet, Feet

Sung to: "Three Blind Mice"

Feet, feet, feet,

Feet, feet, feet.

They're so neat,

They're so neat.

I love to march,

I love to stomp.

I love to walk,

I love to romp.

I love to slide,

I love to clomp.

Feet, feet, feet.

Act out the song movements with your child as you sing.

Jean Warren

Talking Foot

Trace around your child's foot on a piece of construction paper. Cut out the shape and draw on a face. Then attach a plastic straw to the back for a handle and encourage your child to use her foot puppet to tell you stories.

Barefoot Moves

Help your child take off her shoes and socks. Put on some music and invite her to dance, hop, tiptoe, and walk—first on a carpeted area, then on a bare floor. Which feels better on her feet?

Watch Me Go

When you go from place to place, ask your child to use her dancing feet, her tiptoe feet, her sliding feet, and so forth. Join in the fun, if you wish.

This Little Piggy

This little piggy

Went to market.

This little piggy

Stayed home.

This little piggy

Had roast beef.

This little piggy

Had none.

And this little piggy

Said, "Wee, wee, wee!"

All the way home.

Gently wiggle each of your child's toes as you recite the rhyme. Start with her big toe and end with her little one.

Traditional

Shoe Match

Place several pairs of your child's shoes in a pile and invite her to find those that match. Let her put the pairs of shoes into separate shoeboxes, if available.

Making Footprints

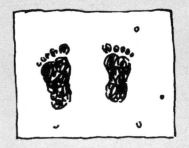

After a bath, let your child make wet footprints on a piece of colored construction paper. Talk about what they look like. What happens to the footprints after a while?

March

Green Forest

Help your child collect outdoor greenery such as leaves, grass, or evergreen sprigs. Brush glue all over a piece of construction paper. Invite your child to arrange his greenery on top of the glue to create a "forest."

Green Grocer

When you take your child grocery shopping, point out green vegetables, such as cucumbers, peppers, broccoli, or lettuce. Let him help you choose one of the veggies to buy and prepare later.

Froggie Hop

Ask your child to get down on his hands and knees, pretending to be a little green frog. Show him how to hop from one make-believe lily pad to another as you make *ribbet* sounds.

Green Snacking

Let your child snack on frozen green peas or green apple slices. Talk about their green color.

Shamrock Plate

Invite your child to attach green shamrock stickers all over a white paper plate. Use the plate for serving snacks on St. Patrick's Day.

Green on Green

Put a piece of green paper or a green towel on the floor. Help your child find green objects, name them, and place them on the paper.

Green, We Love You

Sung to: "Skip to My Lou"

Green, we love you,

Yes, we do.

Green, we love you,

Yes, we do.

Green, we love you,

Yes, we do.

Grass and trees,

And lettuce, too!

Substitute the names of other green things, such as *celery* or *my shirt*, for *lettuce.*

Jean Warren

A Little Bird

Once I saw a little bird
Go hop, hop, hop,
And I called, "Little bird,
Will you stop, stop, stop?"
I was opening the window
To say "How do you do,"
But he shook his little tail,
And far away he flew.

Let your child pretend to be the little bird as you recite the rhyme.

Adapted Traditional

Bird Watching

Take your child on an early-morning walk to look for birds and listen to their songs. What birds are common in your area? Help your child learn a few of their names.

I'm a Birdie

Sung to: "Frère Jacques"

I'm a birdie, I'm a birdie
In the sky, in the sky.
Watch me flying this way,
Watch me flying that way,
Up so high, up so high.

As you sing, pretend to be birds flying in the sky.

Elizabeth McKinnon

Feather Painting

Cut a large bird shape out of construction paper. Let your child use a feather (available at craft stores) to paint on the shape. Encourage her to stick the feather onto her bird shape while the paint is still wet.

Paper Wings

Cut wing shapes out of newspaper and tape them to your child's long sleeves. Encourage her to "fly" around, indoors or out.

Bird Feeding

After lunch or snacktime, look for leftover crumbs. Help your child sweep them up and scatter them outside for the birds.

Birds on a Cloud

For a fun snack, fill a piece of celery with a cream cheese "cloud." Let your child top the cloud with several raisin "birds."

April

Hunting for Eggs

Sung to: "The Mulberry Bush"

Here we go hunting all around,

All around, all around.

Here we go hunting all around

To find our colored eggs.

Substitute other words, such as *walking*, *hopping*, or *tiptoeing*, for *hunting*.

Micki Nadort

Egg Play

Give your child a six-cup egg carton and six plastic eggs. Invite him to try putting the eggs into the cups of the egg carton and taking them out again.

Egg Roll

With your child, curl up on the floor and pretend to be little eggs. Then roll around the room, trying not to bump into each other and "crack your shells." Continue as long as you like.

Rocking Egg

To make this fun toy, place a small amount of sand inside a plastic egg, hot-glue the two halves closed, then use permanent markers to draw on a face and clothing. Let your child rock the toy back and forth or float it in a tub of water.

Egg Hunt

Hide a few plastic eggs or colored-paper egg shapes around the room where your child can easily find them. Give him a small basket with a handle. Help him look for the eggs to place in his basket, singing "Hunting for Eggs" as you search.

Egg Snacks

Throughout the week at snacktime, serve eggs prepared in various ways, such as scrambled, fried, hard-cooked, or deviled.

Egg Surprise

Hide a small toy inside a large plastic egg. Holding the egg in your hand, tell your child a little story about the toy without naming it. At the end, open the egg to reveal the toy's identity.

Peekaboo Basket

Hide a plastic egg or a small toy in a basket and cover it with a cloth. Let your child touch the cloth, try to guess what the object is, then peek under the cloth to see if her guess was correct.

Art Baskets

Each day, give your child a basket filled with different art supplies. For instance, include paper and crayons one day, modeling dough another day, and stickers and paper a third day. Encourage her to create as she wishes.

Baby Doll Basket

Line a basket with a doll blanket or a dishtowel and place a baby doll inside. Explain to your child that the doll needs someone to care for it. Show her how to hold and cuddle the doll, speak to it softly, and sing it a favorite lullaby.

Riding Basket

Invite your child to sit inside a large, sturdy basket, such as a laundry basket. Push her around the room as she gives you directions such as, "Go to the chair. Go faster. Go round and round."

In & Out Basket

Help your child toss rolled-up socks into a basket. Encourage her to say "In!" each time a sock lands inside. Then have her say "Out!" as she tosses the socks out of the basket.

Shopping Basket

Arrange several familiar toys or other objects on a shelf as if in a store. Give your child a basket with a handle and ask her to go shopping for you. Give her directions such as, "Buy one red block. Buy a shiny spoon. Buy a toy car." Continue until all the items have been "purchased."

In My Basket

Sung to: "Twinkle, Twinkle, Little Star"

In my basket you will find
Toys of almost every kind.
Here's a ___ and here's a ___.
Here's a ___ and here's a ___.
In my basket you will find
Toys of almost every kind.

Put four toys into a basket. As you sing, pull out the toys one at a time and let your child name them to fill in the blanks.

Gayle Bittinger

April

Picking Purple

Cut purple pictures out of magazines. Help your child name the items pictured. Then let him pick the pictures he wants and glue them onto a piece of purple paper any way he wishes.

Purple Artwork

Give your child a piece of lavender construction paper and invite him to draw on it with a purple crayon or marker. If you have purple yarn on hand, let him glue on a few short pieces to add to his creation.

Purple Parade

Put on purple by adorning yourself, your child, and favorite stuffed toys with purple ribbons or streamers. Then put on some rousing music and march together around the room in a Purple Parade.

Purple Story

Make up a simple "purple story" and tell it to your child. As you do so, illustrate it with a purple crayon or marker.

Purple Puppet

Cut a circle out of purple paper and draw on a funny face. Add purple paper strips for arms and legs, if you wish. Attach the puppet to a craft stick and use it while singing "I Have a Purple Puppet."

Grape Snacks

At snacktime, serve your child purple grape juice, or toast spread with purple grape jelly. Or, make grape finger gelatin and cut out fun purple shapes with cookie cutters.

I Have a Purple Puppet

Sung to: "If You're Happy and You Know It"

Oh, I have a purple puppet

In my hand.

Oh, I have a purple puppet

In my hand.

Yes, I have a purple puppet,

See me hop it, see me jump it!

Oh, I have a purple puppet

In my hand.

As you sing, use your Purple Puppet to act out the movements described.

Elizabeth McKinnon

Rain Falling Down

Sung to: "Row, Row, Row Your Boat"

Rain, rain falling down,

Falling all around.

What a lovely sound you make,

Splashing on the ground!

Sing with your child on a rainy day.

Susan Moon

Rain Gear

As you get your child ready to go out on a rainy day, help her name each of her rain gear items, such as her rain hat, rain boots, and umbrella. Talk about how each item helps keep her dry.

Puddle Splash

Outdoors, let your child splash through puddles in her rain boots. Indoors, encourage her to show you how she can jump, splash, march, or tiptoe through pretend puddles.

Sidewalk Art

After a rainfall, take your child outdoors and draw on the wet sidewalk with colored chalk. The water will help create vibrant colors.

Showers and Flowers

Teach your child the saying "April showers bring May flowers." Talk about how flowers and other plants need rain in order to grow.

Pitter-Patter

Pitter-patter falls the rain

On the roof and windowpane.

Softly, softly it comes down,

Pitter-patter on the ground.

Show your child how to make soft tapping sounds with her fingers as you recite the rhyme.

Adapted Traditional

Rain Music

Place a bucket or a large tin container upside down in the rain. Invite your child to listen to the music the raindrops make as they fall on the bucket or container.

May

Flowers Blooming

Sung to: "Mary Had a Little Lamb"

Flowers blooming everywhere,
Everywhere, everywhere.
Flowers blooming everywhere,
What a lovely day!

Flowers blooming everywhere,
Everywhere, everywhere.
Flowers blooming everywhere,
In the month of May.

Sing together as you walk by blooming flowers.

Jean Warren

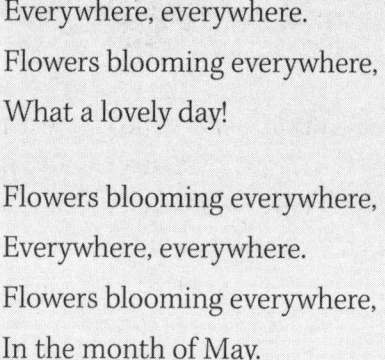

May Basket

Give your child flower stickers to attach to a small paper doily. Then tape the ends of a ribbon handle to opposite edges of the doily to create an instant "flower basket."

Flower Walk

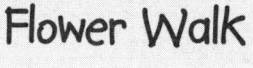

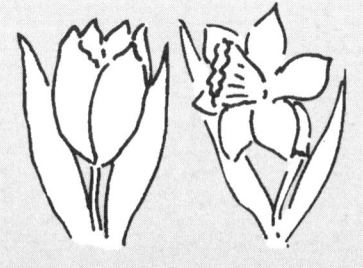

Walk around the neighborhood with your child to look for spring flowers. When you get home, pretend to tiptoe through the tulips, crawl through the carnations, or dance through the daffodils.

Flower Prints

Give your child some dandelions or other flowers with sturdy blossoms. Show him how to make prints by dipping the blossoms into tempera paint and lightly pressing them onto paper. For added fun, cut the paper into flower shapes first.

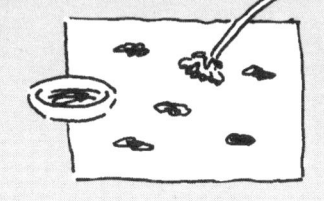

Flower Scents

Take your child to a flower garden and sniff some of the scented blooms. Which does he like best? Or, give your child a cologne-scented cotton ball to glue in the center of a paper flower shape. Encourage him to sniff the scent.

A Flower

My hand is a bud
Closed up tight,
   (Close hand into fist.)
Without a tiny
Speck of light.
Then slowly the petals
Open for me,
   (Slowly open hand.)
And here is a
Beautiful flower I see!

Adapted Traditional

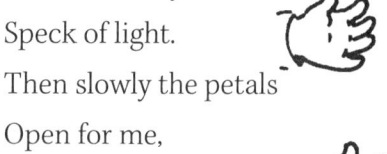

Snacktime Flowers

Cut flower shapes out of various colors of construction paper. Each day this week, hide a different shape under your child's snack plate for him to discover and decorate later.

Caterpillar Storybook

Look in your local children's library or bookstore for a caterpillar picture book to read to your child. A favorite is Eric Carle's *The Very Hungry Caterpillar.*

Caterpillar Search

Look outdoors for caterpillars and encourage your child to examine them. What color are they? How do they move? Or, show your child pictures of caterpillars from books. Explain that later, the caterpillars will turn into butterflies or moths.

Yarn Caterpillar

Cut a large leaf shape from green construction paper and invite your child to decorate it with a green crayon or marker. Then give her a piece of thick yarn, about 4 inches long, to glue on the leaf for a "caterpillar."

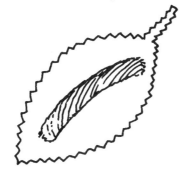

Caterpillar

Caterpillar
Creep.
Caterpillar
Crawl.
Caterpillar
Wiggle
All along the wall.

Crawl your fingers on your child's arm as you recite the rhyme.

Beverly Qualheim

Snacking Caterpillar

For a snack, serve vegetable sticks or fruit slices. Let your child pretend to be a hungry little caterpillar as she nibbles.

Wiggling Caterpillar

Invite your child to stretch out on a rug, pretending to be a caterpillar on a leaf. Encourage her to crawl and wiggle from one end of the leaf to the other. As she does so, sing "Caterpillar, Caterpillar."

Caterpillar, Caterpillar

Sung to: "Frère Jacques"

Caterpillar, caterpillar
On the wall, on the wall.
First you wiggle this way,
Then you wiggle that way.
Crawl, crawl, crawl.
Crawl, crawl, crawl.

Have your child pretend to be a caterpillar as you sing.

Elizabeth McKinnon

May

Exploring Dirt

Dig up a cupful of dirt and place it in a shallow container. Show your child how to use a magnifying glass to examine the dirt. Can he tell you what he sees?

Making Mud

Place some dirt in a dishpan. Invite your child to add water, then stir and observe as the dirt turns into mud. Provide him with small pans and kitchen gadgets to use for mud play.

Mud Stew

While your child is playing with mud, encourage him to cook up some pretend stew. Invite him to put mud into an old pan and add grass, leaves, and so forth for "ingredients." Let him spoon the stew into small pans for serving, if he wishes.

Mud Cake

On a sunny day, turn a round plastic container upside down and let your child pat thin mud all over the bottom and sides to make a "cake." Allow the cake to "bake" dry in the sun. What does it look like when it's done?

Planting in Dirt

Let your child spoon potting soil into a plastic cup. Help him plant a few fast-growing seeds, such as popcorn kernels or dried beans that have been soaked overnight. Invite him to sprinkle on water, place the cup on a sunny windowsill, and wait for sprouts to appear in a few days.

Chocolate Mud Snack

For snacktime, make chocolate pudding "mud." Sprinkle on "dirt" made from chocolate cookie crumbs.

I Love Dirt

Sung to: "Three Blind Mice"

I love dirt,

I love dirt.

Fun brown dirt,

Fun brown dirt.

I love to dig down

In the ground.

I love to have dirt

All around.

I love to pile it

In a mound.

I love dirt!

Sing while your child is playing in the dirt.

Gayle Bittinger

Barnyard Voices

Sung to: "The Paw-Paw Patch"

Cluck, cluck, says the hen.

Cluck, cluck, says the hen.

Cluck, cluck, says the hen.

Way down yonder

In the big barnyard.

Additional verses: Moo, moo, says the cow; Oink, oink, says the pig; Quack, quack, says the duck; Neigh, neigh, says the horse; Baa, baa, says the lamb.

Elizabeth McKinnon

Follow the Mommy Duck

Take the part of a mother duck and invite your child to be your duckling. Play Follow the Leader and have her walk behind you, imitating everything you do. Be sure to waddle and quack as you go!

My Own Barn

With your child, paint a large cardboard box red to make a barn. Let her pretend to be a farmer and play inside her barn with toy farm animals.

Pig Play

Place a mat on the floor for a "mud puddle." Invite your child to lie on the mat and pretend to be a pig taking a cool mud bath. Encourage her to oink and squeal as she rolls around.

Frolicking Lamb

Have your child pretend to be a lamb while you take the part of her mother. Let her dance, leap, and frolic around in her pretend meadow. Whenever you say, "Time to sleep!" have her stop and rest. When you say, "Wake up!" have her start frolicking again.

Treats From Bossie

Talk with your child about all the good foods we get from cows—milk, cheese, butter, ice cream, yogurt, and cottage cheese. Let her help choose a different "Bossie treat" to enjoy each day for a snack.

What Do They Say?

Read your child a picture book about farm animals. Whenever you mention an animal name, encourage her to make that animal's sound—a moo for a cow, an oink for a pig, a neigh for a horse, and so forth.

June

Yes, It's Yellow

Sung to: "London Bridge"

Andrew has a yellow truck,

Yellow truck, yellow truck.

Andrew has a yellow truck.

Yes, it's yellow.

Substitute your child's name for *Andrew* and a yellow item that he has for *truck*.

Elizabeth McKinnon

Dandelions

Take your child for a walk to look for dandelions. Help him pick enough to make a small, yellow bouquet to use at home as a table decoration.

Yellow Dough

Add yellow food coloring to modeling dough, or find some yellow clay. Give your child cookie cutters—yellow, if available—and invite him to enjoy some yellow play

Tasty Fingerpaint

Put a generous amount of lemon pudding on a washable surface. Encourage your child to finger-paint with the tasty yellow "paint."

Traffic Signs and Signals

With your child, look for yellow traffic signs and talk about what they mean. Whenever you are in traffic and the light turns yellow, call out together, "Yellow means slow!"

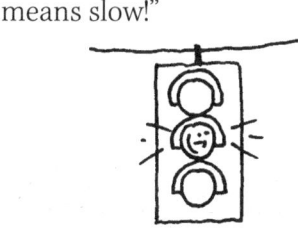

Cornmeal Fun

Put some yellow cornmeal into a large plastic container and talk about its color. Then invite your child to play in the cornmeal with plastic measuring cups and spoons.

Yellow Snacks

Serve your child yellow snacks such as banana pudding or pineapple. Or give him chunks of banana with the skin still on and have him peel off the yellow before eating.

Paper Plate Sun

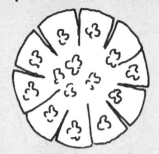

Invite your child to make a sun by tearing yellow paper into small pieces and gluing them all over a small paper plate. When the glue has dried, cut slits around the edge of the plate to create sun rays.

Sunshine Clothes

In a pile, place several of your child's winter and summer clothing items. For instance, include mittens, a down jacket, a bathing suit, and a pair of sandals. Help her sort out the clothes she would wear in the hot sun.

Golden Sunlight

When golden sunlight

Shines on me,

I'm warm and happy

As can be.

Recite the rhyme when you are out in the warm sunshine.

Susan Hodges

Sun and Shadows

Go outdoors on a sunny day to observe shadows. Have your child dance around in the sunlight and watch as her shadow dances along with her. Can she make her shadow touch yours?

Yellow Sun

Cut a large sun shape out of yellow paper and place it on the floor. Set out small yellow toys or other items for your child to discover. When she does so, encourage her to place the items on the yellow sun shape.

Sun Tea

Fill a quart jar with water and let your child add two herbal tea bags (fruit-flavored tea works well). Screw on the lid and put the jar outside in the sun for about three hours. Serve the tea over ice and sweeten to taste.

Sun Is Shining

Sung to: "Clementine"

Sun is shining,

Sun is shining,

Sun is shining

On the grass.

Sun is shining,

Sun is shining,

Sun is shining

On the grass.

As you sing, let your child substitute different words for *grass*.

Diane Thom

June

Beginning Ball Fun

Even young toddlers will enjoy this easy, outdoor ball game. Let your child throw a ball, then have him run after it. When he picks up the ball, encourage him to throw it again. Let him continue the game as long as he likes.

Roll It to Me

For this simple ball game, sit on the floor across from your child with legs outstretched. Roll the ball to your child, then have him roll it back to you. Sing "Roll the Ball" as you play.

Bowling Fun

Invite your child to build several block towers. Have him stand back a few feet, and give him a large, soft ball such as a beach ball. Then let him roll the ball toward the towers to try to knock them over.

Roll the Ball

Sung to: "Row, Row, Row Your Boat"

Roll, roll, roll the ball,

Roll it right to me.

Then I'll roll it back to you

As quick as quick can be!

Sing while rolling a ball back and forth.

Jean Warren

Basket Ball

Set out a laundry basket and give your child a large, soft ball. Together, stand back from the basket and take turns trying to toss the ball into it.

Indoor Ball Fun

Invite your child to experiment with different kinds of balls that can be tossed around indoors. For instance, let him play with rolled-up sock balls, crumpled paper balls, or foam balls.

I'm Bouncing

I'm bouncing, bouncing
(Bounce up and down.)

Everywhere.

I bounce and bounce

Into the air.

I'm bouncing, bouncing

Like a ball.

I bounce and bounce

Until I fall.
(Fall to floor.)

Show your child how to bounce like a ball as you recite the rhyme.

Adapted Traditional

Round the Pillow Patch

Sung to: "The Mulberry Bush"

Here we go round
The pillow patch,
The pillow patch,
The pillow patch.
Here we go round
The pillow patch,
So early in the morning.

Now let's jump
In the pillow patch,
The pillow patch,
The pillow patch.
Now let's jump
In the pillow patch,
So early in the morning.

Substitute such words as *hop* or *crawl* for *jump*.

Jean Warren

Make a Pillow

Let your child help you crumple squares of newspaper and stuff them into a large trash bag. When the bag is full, tie it closed and invite your child to have fun jumping on her big "pillow." (Remember to put the bag away when the game is over.)

Peekaboo Pillow

As your child watches, use one hand to play with a small toy. Gradually move the toy under a pillow, then remove your hand, leaving the toy behind. Can your child guess where the toy is? Encourage her to search for it. Play the game as often as you like.

Flannelboard Pillow

Trace around cookie cutters on pieces of felt and cut out the shapes. Let your child play with the shapes on a textured pillow, arranging them and moving them around as she wishes. Can she tell you a story about the shapes?

Pillow Scoot

Place a pillow on a bare floor and invite your child to sit on it. Show her how to hold onto the front edges of the pillow and use her feet to scoot herself around. Can she scoot forward? Backward? In a circle?

Pillow Picnic

Place pillows on the floor for you and your child to sit on while having a snack. Arrange the pillows into different shapes for a different kind of Pillow Picnic experience each day.

Pillow Patch

Place a big pile of pillows on the floor to make a Pillow Patch. With your child, walk around the pillows and then jump into them. As you do so, sing "Round the Pillow Patch."

July

Paper Plates

Sung to: "Jingle Bells"

Paper plates, paper plates,

Fill them up with treats.

Apple slices, sandwiches,

Oh, so good to eat!

Paper plates, paper plates,

Add some pickles, too.

See the plates all filled up now,

Just for me and you.

Sing as you and your child put foods on paper plates, substituting the names of your foods for those mentioned.

Elizabeth McKinnon

Fourth of July Hat

For a patriotic hat, make a cut from the edge of a thin paper plate to the center, roll the plate into a cone shape, and secure the edges with tape. Help your child decorate the hat with red and blue marker designs and ribbon streamers. Add yarn or ribbon ties to complete.

Plate Toss

For a fun outdoor game, show your child how to toss a small paper plate so that it sails through the air. If you wish, place a blanket on the ground and encourage him to try tossing the plate onto it.

Holiday Plates

Help your child attach red and blue star stickers to white paper plates. Use the plates for serving snacks on the Fourth of July.

Happy or Sad?

Draw a happy face on one side of a paper plate and a sad face on the other side. Use the plate as a puppet for telling your child stories.

Floating Boat

Put a ball of modeling dough in the center of a wax-covered paper plate. Stand a craft stick in the dough for a mast and attach a square paper sail. Float the boat in water and encourage your child to blow on the sail or create waves to make the boat go.

Spaghetti Art

Tint cooked spaghetti with food coloring and place it in a bowl. Let your child arrange the noodles on a paper plate in designs any way he wishes. As the spaghetti dries, the starch in the noodles will help the strands stick to the plate.

Small Sandbox

For a sandbox that can be used indoors or outside, fill a deep plastic dishpan with clean sand. Give your child sand-play toys, such as spoons, funnels, plastic measuring cups, and empty plastic containers. Put an old sheet or shower curtain under the sandbox for indoor play.

Sand Comb

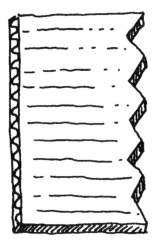

To make this sandbox toy, cut a rectangle out of heavy card-board. On one of the long sides, cut a set of "teeth." Invite your child to use the rectangle to comb patterns in the sand.

Sand Alternatives

If sand is not available, you can use other materials to make a sandbox. Just fill a plastic tub partway with dried split peas, uncooked rice, or dried corn. (Be sure to supervise your child to make sure she doesn't put the materials in her mouth.)

Digging for Treasure

Show your child a shell or a small plastic toy and have her close her eyes while you hide it in her sandbox. When she opens her eyes, encourage her to dig for the "buried treasure." Then let her hide treasure for you to find.

Sand Drawing

Put about an inch of sand in the bottom of a dishpan or a sturdy box. Let your child use a finger to draw designs in the sand. Then show her how to gently shake the pan back and forth to erase so that she can start over again.

Wet Sand Fun

Add a little water to a small sandbox to make damp sand. Give your child cookie cutters and small plastic cups or other containers to use for molding play. Also encourage her to make handprints and footprints in the sand.

I Love Sand

Sung to: "Three Blind Mice"

Sand, sand, sand.

Sand, sand, sand.

I love sand,

I love sand.

It's fun to squish it

Between my toes,

Or build a mountain

As high as my nose,

Or dig a tunnel

That grows and grows,

'Cause I love sand!

Sing while your child is playing in sand.

Susan Hodges

July

Blue Snacking Fun

At snacktime, serve yogurt topped with blueberries. Or, let your child help you make blue gelatin.

Picture Book Blues

Look at a picture book or a magazine with your child. Help him find and name as many blue things as he can.

I See Blue

Sung to: "Frère Jacques"

I see blue, I see blue,

Yes I do, yes I do.

I see a blue crayon,

I see a blue block.

I see blue, yes I do.

Encourage your child to substitute the names of blue things he sees for *crayon* and *block*.

Elizabeth McKinnon

Blue Blot Picture

Fold a piece of white construction paper in half and then open it. Help your child squirt on a drop of blue food coloring. Refold the paper, let your child rub across it, then open the paper to reveal the Blue Blot Picture inside.

Blue Note

Use a blue pen to write a card to send to a relative or a friend. Let your child add a blue scribble. Then together, take the card to a blue mailbox and send it on its way.

Building With Blue

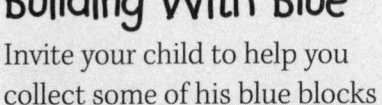

Invite your child to help you collect some of his blue blocks or other building toys. Together, try building a structure with them. Talk about the color blue as you build.

Little Boy Blue

Little Boy Blue,

Come blow your horn.

The sheep's in the meadow,

The cow's in the corn.

But where is the boy

Who looks after the sheep?

He's under the haystack,

Fast asleep.

Let your child pretend to be Little Boy Blue as you recite the rhyme.

Adapted Traditional

Oh, I Wish I Had a Sponge

Sung to: "Twinkle, Twinkle, Little Star"

Oh, I wish I had a sponge.

I know I'd have lots of fun.

I could wipe and wipe all day.

I could squeeze it when I play.

Oh, I wish I had a sponge.

I know I'd have lots of fun.

Sing when you're getting ready for sponge play.

Jean Warren

Sorting Fun

Find two sponges of different colors and cut them both into fourths. Mix up the sponge pieces and help your child sort them by color. Save the pieces to use as Sponge Blocks, if you wish.

Sponge Puzzles

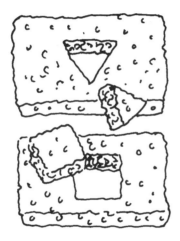

Find two or three large, flat sponges. Using a craft knife, cut a simple shape out of the center of each sponge to make a puzzle. Show your child how to play with the puzzles by taking the shapes out of the sponges and putting them back in again.

Sponge Blocks

Give your child whole sponges and sponges cut into smaller shapes to use as blocks. Let her experiment with building while the blocks are wet as well as dry. What differences does she notice?

Sponge Painting

Pour tempera paint into a shallow container. Invite your child to dip small sponge pieces into the paint and press them onto paper to make prints. Or, encourage her to use the sponges like brushes to paint designs on the paper.

Wet Sponge Toss

On a hot day, place a bucket of water and a sponge in an outdoor area. Invite your child to join you in a game of catch using the wet sponge. Dressing in bathing suits or shorts makes the game extra-refreshing.

I'm a Helper

Let your child use a damp or dry sponge to wipe various surfaces, such as your kitchen tabletop, chair seats, woodwork, or vinyl floor. Be sure to thank her for being such a good helper.

August

Out in the Yard

Sung to: "Twinkle, Twinkle, Little Star"

Let's go out

In the yard and play.

The sun is shining,

It's a beautiful day.

We will hop

And skip and run.

We will have

A lot of fun.

Let's go out

In the yard and play.

The sun is shining,

It's a beautiful day.

Sing before going outdoors to play.

Patricia Coyne

Painting With Water

Give your child a bucket of water and a big paintbrush. Invite him to use the water to "paint" surfaces or objects around the yard, such as an outside wall, a fence, or a picnic table.

Story Hour

Find a shady spot in your yard for reading stories. Let your child bring out a few of his stuffed toys to listen with him as you read aloud favorite picture books.

Outdoor Picnic

Let your child help you pack picnic lunches into small paper bags. Include such foods as sandwiches, fruit slices, or boxed juice. Then together, find a cozy spot in your yard to enjoy your Outdoor Picnic.

Grass Picture

Let your child pick several handfuls of grass. Brush glue over a piece of construction paper and invite him to sprinkle the grass on top of the glue. Help him attach a few animal stickers to complete his picture, if you wish.

Hose Play

On a hot day, turn on the sprinkler and run through it with your child. For added fun, show him how to fold or twist the hose in the middle to make the water stop and start again.

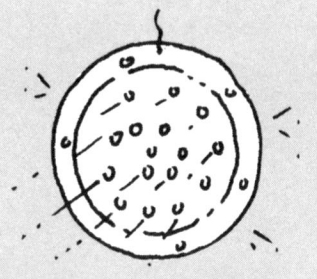

Magical Mobiles

Use a hammer and a nail to punch designs in throwaway aluminum pie pans. Hang the pans in your yard where your child can watch them as they spin and sparkle in the sun.

Bell Ring

Use pieces of yarn to hang two bells from a tree branch, one up high and one down low, both within your child's reach. Let her try touching the bells, first to make the high one ring, then to ring the low one.

Musical Highs and Lows

With your child, choose a familiar song such as "Mary Had a Little Lamb." Sing it first in high voices, then in low voices. Follow up by playing high and low notes on a piano or other instrument.

High Spray, Low Spray

Take your child outdoors and give her a small spray bottle filled with water. Have her spray the water high and low on surfaces such as a fence or an outside wall.

Reaching High and Low

Sung to: "Here We Go Looby Loo"

I can reach up so high,

I can reach down so low.

I can reach up so high

As round and round we go.

Walk in a slow circle and act out the movements as you sing.

Elizabeth McKinnon

High Shelf, Low Shelf

Invite your child to help you arrange objects on a two-shelf bookcase or toy cabinet. Give her directions such as, "Put the red blocks on the high shelf. Now put the kitty book on the low shelf."

Swinging High and Low

Take your child to a playground and give her a ride on a swing. As you gently push her, chant, "High, low, high, low. Brooke swings high, Brooke swings low." Substitute your child's name for *Brooke*.

Bouncing

Bouncing, bouncing,

Bouncing high.

Bouncing, bouncing

To the sky.

Bouncing, bouncing,

Bouncing low.

Bouncing, bouncing,

Down I go.

Bounce high, then low as you recite the rhyme.

Elizabeth McKinnon

August

Mix With Water

Let your child help you measure water and mix it with juice concentrate as directed on the container. Serve the juice with ice for a snacktime drink.

Water Tub

Fill a plastic dishpan with water. Provide your child with water-play toys, such as plastic measuring cups, a sponge, a funnel, a turkey baster, and a squeeze bottle. Encourage him to use the toys for pouring, squeezing, and squirting. (Remember to supervise all water play.)

Doing the Laundry

Add a squirt of mild liquid hand soap to your child's Water Tub. Invite him to wash baby clothes or washcloths in the soapy water. Then let him rinse the items and hang them up to dry.

Water Sprinkler

Make a sprinkler for your child to use in his Water Tub. Poke holes around the lower part of a yogurt cup or a similar container. Invite your child to fill the cup with water and watch it pour out through the holes.

Sink or Float?

Give your child heavy and light objects to play with in his Water Tub. Suggestions include a rock, a metal spoon, a ring of keys, a leaf, a sponge, and a plastic toy. Let him try to guess which objects will sink and which will float before he puts them into the water.

Car Wash

Let your child help you use a hose to fill a bucket with water. Then give him a sponge and invite him to use the materials to wash his trike, wagon, or other big toys.

Water, Water

Sung to: "Twinkle, Twinkle, Little Star"

Water, water everywhere,

On my face and on my hair.

On my fingers, on my toes.

On my ears and on my nose.

Water, water everywhere,

On my face and on my hair.

As you sing, point to the parts of the body mentioned.

Jean Warren

Out in the Garden

Sung to: "Down by the Station"

Out in the garden,

Early in the morning,

See the red tomatoes

All in a row.

See the happy farmer

Coming out to pick them.

Pick, pick, pick, pick.

Off she goes.

Continue with verses about orange carrots, yellow squashes, green string beans, and purple cabbages. Let your child pretend to be the farmer as you sing.

Jean Warren

In the Bag

Set out sturdy vegetables, such as potatoes, carrots, zucchini, and corn on the cob. Help your child name the veggies as she puts them into a grocery bag and takes them out again.

Veggie Soup

Let your child help wash and scrub fresh vegetables for making soup. Suggestions include potatoes, tomatoes, onions, carrots, and celery. Cut up the veggies, invite your child to put them into a pot, then add broth and simmer until tender. Serve for lunch or dinner.

Veggie Prints

Make paint pads by placing folded paper towels in two shallow containers and pouring on different colors of tempera paint. Cut a potato or a zucchini in half. Show your child how to press the cut ends of the vegetable pieces onto the paint pads, then onto paper to make prints.

Hi, Mr. Potato

Cut eyes, a nose, and a mouth in the side of a potato. Cut a deep finger hole in the bottom. Poke a finger up through the middle of a paper napkin and into the finger hole in the potato to create a puppet with a paper jacket. Use the puppet for singing songs or telling stories.

Veggie Plate

Cut pictures of vegetables out of a seed catalog or a magazine. Help your child brush glue onto a paper plate. Then let her arrange the pictures on top of the glue any way she wishes.

Veggie Snack

Cut vegetables, such as carrots, celery, or cucumbers, into sticks. Serve the veggies with a favorite dip at snacktime.

September

Easy Sticking

Make working with stickers easier for your child by removing them from their backing and lightly attaching them to a piece of waxed paper. Show your child how the stickers can be removed and attached over and over again.

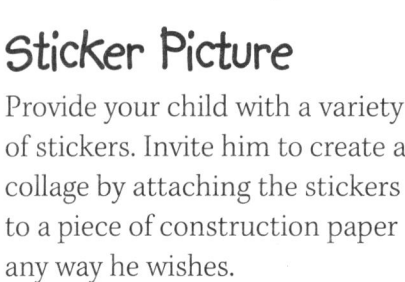

Sticker Picture

Provide your child with a variety of stickers. Invite him to create a collage by attaching the stickers to a piece of construction paper any way he wishes.

Sticker Directions

Attach a sticker to your child's index finger. Give him directions such as, "Dance your sticker in the air" or "Touch your sticker to your toe." Then attach a sticker to your finger and encourage your child to give you directions.

Sticker Crown

Cut a crown shape out of construction paper and have your child decorate it with stickers. Then fit the crown around his head, tape the ends in place, and let him wear his crown as long as he likes.

Decorated Snack Cup

Give your child a small paper cup and help him decorate it with stickers. Then fill the cup with pieces of fruit or other finger food for a snack.

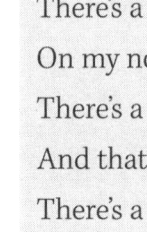

Puppet Fun

For an easy puppet, attach a character sticker, such as a bear or a duck, to a craft stick or a finger. With your child, sing songs or tell stories about the character while moving the puppet around.

There's a Sticker on My Nose

Sung to: "If You're Happy and You Know It"

There's a sticker on my nose,

On my nose.

There's a sticker on my nose,

On my nose.

There's a sticker on my nose,

And that's the way it goes.

There's a sticker on my nose,

On my nose.

Attach stickers to your noses before singing.

Jean Warren

Found a Beanbag

Sung to: "Clementine"

Found a beanbag,

Found a beanbag,

Found a beanbag

Just now.

Just now I

Found a beanbag,

Found a beanbag

Just now.

Place beanbags around on the floor. Sing as you and your child pick them up.

Adapted Traditional

Beanbags

Purchase a variety of beanbags for your child to play with. Or, make your own by filling small socks with dried beans and securely sewing the socks closed. Check beanbags often for rips or tears that need repairing.

Easy Beanbags

For quick and easy beanbags, fill pint-size resealable plastic bags with dried peas or navy beans. Seal the bags and secure them with heavy tape. Or, stuff the bags with old nylons or cotton balls for soft beanbags.

Beanbag Balance

Place a beanbag on your child's head or on top of her shoe. How far can she walk before the beanbag falls off? Play the game along with her, if you like.

Beanbag Toss

Sit on the floor across from your child. Gently toss a beanbag to her and have her toss it back. Continue tossing and catching as long as you wish, reciting "A Beanbag" as you do so.

A Beanbag

Here is a beanbag,

I'll toss it to you.

Please catch it and toss it

Right back to me, too.

Recite while tossing a beanbag back and forth.

Adapted Traditional

Beanbag Drop

Place a laundry basket on the floor and let your child try dropping beanbags into it. As her tossing skills develop, move the basket farther away. Or, for a special challenge, substitute a pot or a pan for the basket.

September

Shake Your Cups

Sung to: "Row, Row, Row Your Boat"

Shake, shake, shake your cups,

Shake them high and low.

Shake them all around the room,

Everywhere you go.

Give your child a Paper Cup Shaker to shake as you sing.

Jean Warren

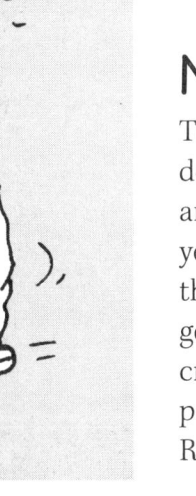

Where's the Cracker?

Place two different-looking paper cups upside down on a table. Ask your child to watch as you put a small cracker under one cup and then move the cups around several times. Can he guess under which cup the cracker is hiding?

Nosie Rosie Puppet

Turn a small paper cup upside down and poke two eye holes and a nose hole in one side. Help your child put his hand up into the cup and stick his index finger out through the nose hole to create a wiggly nose for his puppet. Ask questions for Nosie Rosie to answer.

Paper Cup Shaker

Put dried beans into a paper cup, place a second cup upside down on top of the first cup, and securely tape the rims together. Encourage your child to shake his shaker as you sing "Shake Your Cups."

Printing Circles

Set out several sizes of paper cups. Make paint pads by placing flat sponges in shallow containers and pouring on tempera paint. Show your child how to press the rims of the cups onto the paint pads and then onto paper to make circle prints.

Frozen Snacks

Freeze juice in small paper cups. Help your child peel down the sides of a cup to eat the frozen juice.

Nesting Cups

Select several sizes of paper cups that fit one inside the other. Show your child how to nest the cups together and take them apart again. Let him play with the cups as long as he likes.

Rake and Jump

Invite your child to help you rake dry autumn leaves into a big pile. Then let her enjoy jumping into the soft, crinkly leaves.

Leaf Rubbing

Fold a fresh leaf inside a piece of lightweight paper. Tape two sides of the paper closed to make an "envelope." Show your child how to rub a peeled crayon across the envelope to make the leaf impression magically appear. Then remove the leaf for her to see.

Leaf Match

Find a leaf on the ground and talk with your child about its shape. Then help her search for other leaves that look just like it.

Falling Leaf

Ask your child to imagine that she is an autumn leaf hanging from a tree branch. Pretend to be the wind and blow her off the tree. Encourage her to twirl and swirl around as she gently falls to the ground.

Leaf Toast

Using a cookie cutter or a knife, cut leaf shapes from pieces of toast. Let your child help add peanut butter or soft cheese spread.

Crinkly Leaf Art

Collect a bowlful of dry autumn leaves. Cut a large leaf shape out of yellow construction paper and help your child brush glue all over it. Then invite her to crumble the dry leaves and sprinkle the pieces on top of the glue.

Leaves, Leaves

Sung to: "Row, Row, Row Your Boat"

Leaves, leaves
Falling down,
Falling on the ground.
Red and yellow,
Orange and brown.
Leaves are falling down.

Sing as you are watching autumn leaves fall.

Susan A. Miller

October

Printing With Orange

Help your child dip a thick round of carrot into orange tempera paint. Show him how to press the carrot onto a piece of white paper to make orange prints.

Sensing Oranges

Invite your child to hold an orange in each hand. What do the oranges look like? Which feels heaviest? Lightest? Peel one of the oranges. What color are the segments? How do they smell? How do they taste?

Orange Snacks

Throughout the week, offer your child a variety of orange-colored snacks. Some suggestions are cantaloupe chunks, peach slices, cheese-flavored crackers, orange segments, cheese cubes, and grated carrots.

Orange Modeling Dough

Stir 3 tablespoons vegetable oil and 1 package unsweetened orange-flavored drink mix into 2 cups boiling water. Set aside. In a bowl, mix 2½ cups flour, 1 cup salt, and 1 tablespoon cream of tartar. Add the water mixture and stir until dough forms. Warm dough is especially fun to play with!

Orange Dancing

Give your child an orange object, such as a toy or a piece of clothing. Then play music and encourage him to dance around the room, holding the orange object in his hand.

I Love Orange

I love the color orange.

Oh yes, oh yes, I do!

It's the color of orange juice

And carrots and pumpkins, too.

Substitute such words as *goldfish* or *my crayon* for *orange juice*.

Jean Warren

Orange, Orange, Orange

Sung to: "Three Blind Mice"

Orange, orange, orange.

Orange, orange, orange.

What is orange?

What is orange?

An orange, a cantaloupe,

And a peach.

A pumpkin, a goldfish,

And Cheddar cheese.

A carrot, and other good

Things to eat—

All are orange.

Let your child color with an orange crayon or marker as you sing.

Diane Thom

See the Pumpkins

Sung to: "Frère Jacques"

See the pumpkins,

See the pumpkins,

Orange and round,

Orange and round.

See the little pumpkins,

See the great big pumpkins,

Orange and round,

Orange and round.

Give your child big and little pumpkin stickers to play with as you sing.

Gayle Bittinger

Choosing a Pumpkin

Visit a pumpkin farm or a supermarket to look at the pumpkins on display. Talk with your child about their color, size, and shape. Then let her help pick out a pumpkin to take home.

Pumpkin Dress-Up

Before carving your pumpkin, use a permanent marker to draw on a face. Set out the pumpkin along with several different hats. Invite your child to dress up the pumpkin by putting the hats on it.

Pumpkin Search

Cut small pumpkin shapes out of orange paper and scatter them around on the floor. Let your child search for the pumpkins and put them into a paper bag. When all the shapes have been found, scatter them again for a new round of the game.

In and Out of the Pumpkin

Let your child enjoy putting small toys into a plastic pumpkin and taking them out again. Ask questions such as, "Is the toy car in or out of the pumpkin? Can you put the block in the pumpkin? Now can you take it out?"

Pumpkin Smoothies

In a blender, whirl together 2 tablespoons cooked pumpkin, 1 cup milk, and 1 sliced banana. Pour into plastic cups for a snacktime treat.

Pumpkin Roll

Pumpkin, pumpkin

On the ground,

Rolling, rolling

All around.

See it rolling

Down the hill—

Now it stops

And lies so still.

Let your child pretend to be a rolling pumpkin as you recite the rhyme.

Elizabeth McKinnon

October

Eyes and Ears

Sung to: "Frère Jacques"

Eyes and ears,

Eyes and ears,

Mouth and nose,

Mouth and nose.

See me touch my eyes,

See me touch my ears,

Then my mouth,

Then my nose.

As you sing, act out the movements with your child.

Adapted Traditional

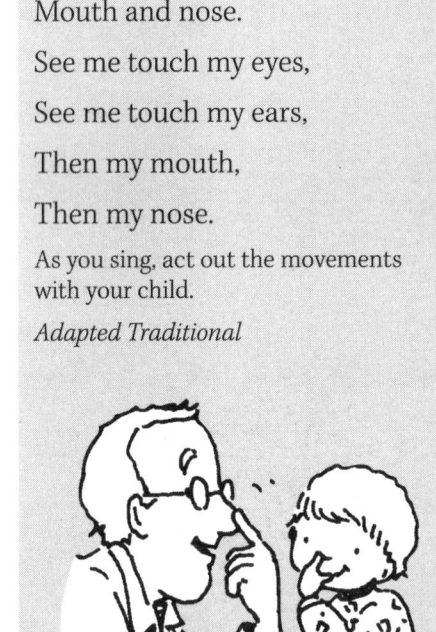

Making Faces

Cut a large circle out of orange felt for a pumpkin. From black felt, cut out several eye, nose, and mouth shapes. Show your child how to arrange the shapes on the pumpkin to create different faces.

Jack-O'-Lanterns

Call your child's attention to jack-o'-lantern faces you see. Do they look happy? Sad? Scary? Encourage him to try mimicking the faces while you join in the fun, too.

Mirror Fun

Look in a mirror with your child. Make a funny face and ask him to try imitating it. Then encourage him to make a face for you to imitate.

Snack Faces

Let your child use a plastic knife to spread peanut butter on round crackers. Then invite him to make faces on the crackers with raisins.

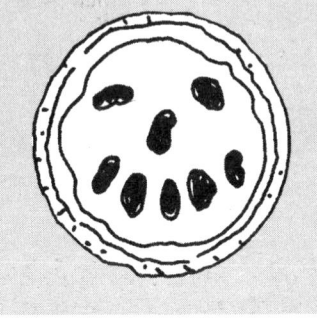

Flashlight Touch

Have your child point as you ask, "Where is your nose? Your mouth?" and so forth. Then hang a picture of a face on a wall and let him shine a small flashlight on the parts of the face as you name them.

Kissy Face

Ask your child to name different parts of his face where he would like you to plant a little kiss. Then you name parts of your face and invite him to give you kisses.

November

Sticker Art

Lightly attach stickers to a piece of waxed paper. Invite your child to take them off the waxed paper and place them on a piece of construction paper to make a collage. Talk about *off* and *on* as your child works.

Movement Square

Tape a square of paper to the floor. Give your child movement directions such as, "Jump on the square. Jump off the square. Put one hand on the square. Put two hands on the square. Take your hands off the square."

On & Off Leaves

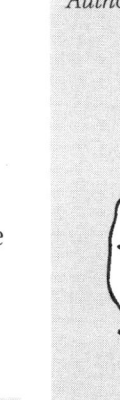

With your child, make a pile of leaves outdoors. Give him directions such as, "Take a leaf off the pile and put it on the stairs. Take another leaf off the pile and put it on the sidewalk."

On & Off Magnets

Give your child a nonaluminum baking sheet for a magnet board. Let him play with magnets, putting them on the board and taking them off. As he does so, say, "The blue magnet is on the board. The yellow magnet is off the board," and so forth.

My Hat

I can put my hat on.

I can take it off.

Watch me put it on my head.

Now watch me take it off.

Take turns putting on a hat and taking it off.

Author Unknown

Mealtime Talk

Take advantage of mealtimes to reinforce your child's understanding of *on* and *off*. For instance, say, "Put on your bib," "Take off your bib," or, "Please take a cracker off the serving plate and put it on your own plate."

A Bow on My Knee

Sung to: "If You're Happy and You Know It"

There's a bow on my knee,

On my knee.

There's a bow on my knee,

On my knee.

There's a bow on my knee,

Now I'll take it off of me.

There's a bow off my knee,

Off my knee.

As you sing, let your child use a self-stick gift-wrap bow to act out the song.

Gayle Bittinger

Dress-Up Box

Set out a box of dress-up clothes for your child to use as simple costumes. For instance, include a cape and a crown for a princess costume, or a red hat and some boots for a firefighter costume. Be sure to have a mirror nearby when helping your child try on outfits.

Costume Song

Sung to: "London Bridge"

Rio has a costume on,

Costume on, costume on.

Rio has a costume on.

She's a pumpkin!

Substitute the name of your child for *Rio* and the name of her costume for *pumpkin*.

Elizabeth McKinnon

Easy Face Paint

Mix a little hand or face lotion with a drop or two of food coloring. Let your child dab the lotion on her nose, cheeks, and chin to create a funny face. This paint is nontoxic and washes off easily with warm water.

Scarf Fun

Help your child make various costumes with scarves. Suggestions include tying a scarf around her head for a hat, tucking several scarves into her waistband for a skirt, or tying scarves to her arms for butterfly wings.

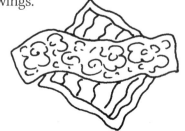

Paper Cloak

Make a simple cloak for your child to wear for a costume by cutting a head hole in the middle of a double page of newspaper. Help her slip the cloak over her shoulders.

Don't Be Scared

Halloween can be a scary time for toddlers. Look for ways to help your child understand that people wearing costumes and masks are just playing dress-up.

I Look in the Mirror

I look in the mirror

And what do I see?

I see a cowgirl

Looking at me.

As your child tries on different costumes, look in the mirror with her and recite the rhyme, substituting the name of her costume for *cowgirl*.

Adapted Traditional

November

Pots & Pans March

Sung to: "The Muffin Man"

Banging on our pots and pans,

Pots and pans, pots and pans,

Banging on our pots and pans,

We march around the room.

As you sing, march around the room, banging on pots and pans with wooden spoons.

Elizabeth McKinnon

Lid Match

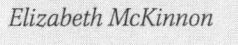

Set out several pots and pans of different sizes along with their lids. Invite your child to try the lids on the pots and pans to find the matchups.

Pretend Cooking

When your child is playing with pots and pans, give him some unopened cans or boxes of food. Encourage him to use the materials to make a pretend meal.

Making Sounds

Line up several pots and pans on the floor. Let your child gently tap them with various objects, such as a wooden spoon, a metal spoon, a pencil, or a plastic straw. Which objects make the loudest sounds? The softest?

Modeling Dough Pies

Make modeling dough by mixing together 1 cup flour, 1/2 cup salt, 1 tablespoon oil, and 6 to 7 tablespoons water. Scent the dough with cinnamon. Then give your child tart pans or other small pans and invite him to make some pretend pies.

One Inside the Other

Find several pots and pans that fit one inside the other. Nest them together and show your child how to take them apart. Then have him try nesting them himself as you offer help as needed.

Washing and Drying

Give your child a dishpan, a dry sponge, small pots and pans, and a dishtowel. Let him pretend to wash the pots and pans and then dry them.

I'm a Cook

Sung to: "Frère Jacques"

I'm a cook, I'm a cook.

See me look in my book.

I can make some pizza,

I can make some cookies.

Watch me cook, watch me cook.

Encourage your child to substitute other words for *pizza* and *cookies*.

Jean Warren

Cinnamon Toast

In a small bowl, mix cinnamon with sugar. Let your child use a plastic knife to spread soft butter on a piece of toast, giving help as needed. Then have her use her fingers to sprinkle the cinnamon sugar on her toast.

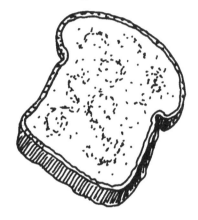

Fruit Salad

Put a spoonful of canned fruit cocktail or pineapple in one small bowl and a dollop of whipped topping in another. Let your child use a plastic knife to slice a piece of banana and add the slices to the canned fruit. Then have her spoon the fruit mixture into the whipped topping.

Take a Dip

Help your child stir a sprinkling of dry ranch dressing into a spoonful of plain yogurt. Then give her vegetable sticks or crackers to dip into her yogurt mixture before eating.

Cheese and Crackers

Place a few crackers on a plate and give your child a plastic knife. Show her how to spread softened cream cheese or another kind of soft cheese spread on the crackers.

Making Pudding

Put 1 tablespoon instant pudding mix and 2 tablespoons milk into a baby food jar and tightly fasten the lid. Have your child shake the jar for about 45 seconds. Then give her a small spoon for eating her pudding right out of the jar.

Frosting Fun

Let your child use a plastic knife to spread soft frosting on graham crackers, muffins, or ready-made cookies. Show her how to add sprinkles for decorations.

December

Holiday Light

Sung to: "I'm a Little Teapot"

I'm a little light bulb
Round and bright.
Here is my twinkle,
Oh, what a sight!
On a holiday
Just plug me in,
And watch me blink
Again and again!

Let your child pretend to be a twinkling holiday bulb as you sing.

Vivian Sasser

Viewing Lights

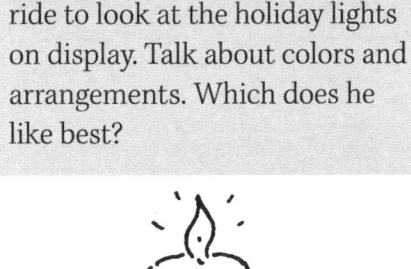

Take your child for a walk or a ride to look at the holiday lights on display. Talk about colors and arrangements. Which does he like best?

Name the Lights

Together, look through magazines to find pictures of various kinds of lights, such as lamps, candles, car lights, and Christmas tree lights. Help your child name the lights you discover.

Flash Dance

Dim the lights in the room and slowly dance the beam of a flashlight across the floor. Invite your child to try jumping or stepping onto the moving beam.

Tree Lights

Cut a small Christmas tree shape from green construction paper and punch holes in it. Show your child how to "light up the tree" by moving it around on a piece of gift-wrap paper so that the various colors appear through the holes.

Switching On and Off

Let your child stand on a sturdy step stool next to a wall light switch. Invite him to move the switch up or down as you call out, "On!" or, "Off!"

Little Light

Twinkle, twinkle,
Little light.
I can see you
Burning bright.

You glow and glow
When you are on,
But when you're off
Your glow is gone.

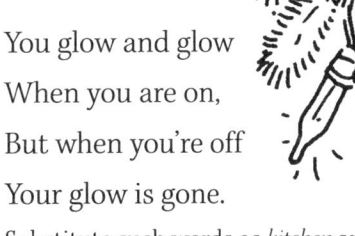

Substitute such words as *kitchen* or *Christmas* for *little*.

Elizabeth McKinnon

Mr. Tape Man

Sung to: "Frère Jacques"

Mr. Tape Man, Mr. Tape Man,

I see you. I see you.

I can see you dancing.

I can see you twirling.

I see you. I see you.

Sing while your child is playing with her Tape Man Puppet.

Elizabeth McKinnon

Wrapping Practice

Give your child tissue paper and small pieces of tape to use for wrapping some of her small toys. Later, have her guess what's inside as she unwraps the "presents."

Tape Pickup

Wrap masking tape sticky-side out around your child's fingers. Let her try using her "sticky hand" to pick up small, lightweight items such as feathers, paper scraps, or snippets of yarn.

Tape Ball

If you find that your child wants to play with tape rather than use it for a project, pull off an extra-long piece and loosely form it into a ball. She can now use the ball for playing and leave the other tape for working.

Tape Collage

Tear masking tape into various lengths and lightly attach the pieces to the rim of your work table. Invite your child to remove the pieces and stick them onto a piece of construction paper any way she wishes to create a collage.

Balance Beam

Attach a long piece of masking tape to the floor. Encourage your child to try walking, crawling, tiptoeing, or hopping along the tape.

Tape Man Puppet

Cover your child's fingertip with masking tape and use a ballpoint pen to draw on a face. Encourage her to use her puppet when she talks to you or when you sing "Mr. Tape Man."

December

Holiday Card

Set out ink pads in holiday colors—blue and yellow for Hanukkah; red and green for Christmas; or red, green, and black for Kwanzaa. Let your child use rubber stamps to print designs all over a piece of white paper. Then fold the paper in half and have him dictate a greeting for you to write inside.

Gift-Wrap Paper

Give your child rubber stamps and colored ink pads. Encourage him to print designs on a piece of large paper, such as butcher paper, brown wrapping paper, or even newspaper. Use the paper to wrap holiday gifts.

Decorated Tree

Cut a large Christmas tree shape out of green construction paper. Show your child how to use rubber stamps and colored ink pads to decorate the tree with printed "ornaments."

Gift Bag

Invite your child to decorate a paper lunch bag with colorful rubber stamp designs. Punch two holes through opposite sides of the top of the bag for inserting a yarn or ribbon tie.

Holiday Wreath

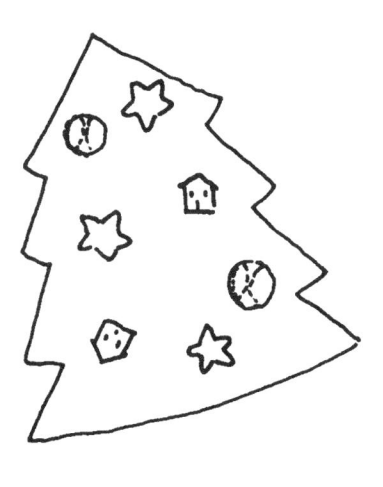

Cut the center out of a small, white paper plate and give the rim to your child. Let him use a rubber stamp and a green ink pad to cover the rim with prints. To complete his wreath, help him attach a red self-stick bow.

Holiday Place Cards

Invite your child to stamp prints in holiday colors onto small index cards. Fold the cards in half, print names on the fronts, and stand them on a table at mealtime.

Stamp Your Stamp

Sung to: "Row, Row, Row Your Boat"

Stamp, stamp,

Stamp your stamp,

Stamp it here and there.

Stamp it, stamp it,

Stamp it, stamp it.

Stamp it everywhere.

Sing while your child is stamping on paper.

Jean Warren

Snacktime Fun

Use a cookie cutter to make turkey-shaped sandwiches for snacktime. Or, make turkey-shaped cookies for your child to help decorate.

Turkey Placemats

Invite your child to help make Thanksgiving placemats. Set out pieces of construction paper in autumn colors and let her attach turkey stickers any way she wishes. Cover the papers with clear self-stick paper, if you like.

Turkey Puppet

Attach a small turkey shape or a turkey sticker to the end of a craft stick. Invite your child to use the puppet when you sing about turkeys or tell turkey stories.

Turkey Strut

Use small pieces of masking tape to make turkey footprints on the floor. Play music and have your child strut around the room. Whenever you stop the music, have her find a footprint to stand on. Continue as long as you like.

Feathered Turkey

Set out a large construction-paper turkey shape along with small feathers from a craft store. Help your child brush glue on the shape and place the feathers on top of the glue. Display the turkey as a holiday decoration.

Gobble, Gobble

A turkey is a funny bird,

Its head goes wobble, wobble.
> (Wobble head.)

It knows just one funny word—

Gobble, gobble, gobble!
> (Make gobbling sounds.)

Lynn Beaird

It's a Lot of Fun

Sung to: "The Farmer in the Dell"

Let's do the turkey hop.
> (Hop.)

Let's do the turkey run.
> (Run in place.)

Let's wobble like a turkey now.
> (Strut around.)

It's a lot of fun!

Diane Thom